100

THINGS TO DO IN
OMAHA
BEFORE YOU
DIE

100
THINGS TO DO IN
OMAHA
BEFORE YOU
DIE

TIM AND LISA TRUDELL

Library of Congress Control Number: 2017934534

ISBN: 9781681060958

Design by Jill Halpin

Printed in the United States of America
18 19 20 21 22   5 4 3 2

DEDICATION

We'd like to dedicate this book in memory of Tim's mom and step-dad, Marvin and Cecil Swanson, and our other relatives who helped pave the paths we each took in our lives.

CONTENTS

• •

● ●

Sports and Recreation

• •

Culture and History

• •

Shopping and Fashion

• •

• •

PREFACE

We're strong supporters of Omaha. When someone asks, "What's there to do in Omaha?" Lisa and I are quick to reply with questions about what they're interested in or would like to do. "There's nothing to do in Omaha." When we hear these words, we'll recommend a list of fun activities or attractions to check out. We love Omaha and are proud of our city.

While not natives, we've each called the city home for more than thirty years. When I left the Air Force, our family wanted to live in Omaha so that our daughters could enjoy a great area to grow up in. It's been fun calling Omaha home, just like famous Omahans Henry Fonda, Fred Astaire, Marlon Brando, Bob Gibson, Warren Buffett, Alexander Payne, and Gabrielle Union.

We've enjoyed watching Omaha grow over the years, from being called a cowtown and flyover city to becoming "the best-kept secret" in the United States. The city is home to several major sporting events each year, from college basketball tournaments to Olympic trials and being the home of the College World Series for decades. Major musical acts love performing before a packed house at the CenturyLink Center.

Every day can be an adventure. What's the new exhibit at the Kaneko art gallery? What's the new feature at the Henry Doorly Zoo and Aquarium? Where's the new restaurant opening? We look forward to exploring Omaha and the new things we'll see and learn.

• •

As Omaha grows, our suburbs grow. Some attractions and restaurants featured in this book are located in the suburbs. Omaha is also known as the "15-minute city" because most areas can be reached in a short drive. Other attractions are located within a 30-minute drive.

Omahans love our steaks and trying new foods. We enjoy our history and art, and our sports. No longer that flyover city, you'll see why Omaha may not stay America's best-kept secret much longer.

ACKNOWLEDGMENTS

Thank you to our family and friends who encouraged us to start our travel blog, The Walking Tourists. Without their encouragement, we wouldn't have achieved our success. Thank you to our daughters, Stephanie and Mallory, who are wonderful women and have also enjoyed traveling. Thank you to our friends with the Midwest Travel Bloggers and our Facebook and Twitter friends for their help with our blogging. Thank you to everyone for choosing to follow us on our adventures. Lisa credits her parents with instilling the travel bug in her, with their moves around the country during her dad's career. As a young kid in small town Kennard, Nebraska, Tim never would have thought he'd travel to the places he has over the years. He appreciates the US Air Force for sending an 18-year-old kid to Germany and opening his eyes to the world.

• •

FOOD AND DRINK

NOTHING BEATS
HOME COOKING

Big Mama's Kitchen and Catering serves up some big dishes. From Big Mama's signature French toast to her famous oven-fried chicken, every dish is a winner. Besides a delicious meal, some diners would also get a sit-down with the chef. Patricia Barron, aka Big Mama, loved cooking and visiting with customers, so it was common for her to join people at their table. Seeking an opportunity to open a family-style diner following her retirement from a local phone company, Big Mama accepted an invitation to open her diner on the campus of the former Nebraska School for the Deaf, taking over the old cafeteria. More than a decade later, Big Mama's keeps turning out delicious plates. The restaurant has been featured on national TV shows, such as *Diners, Drive-Ins and Dives.*

3223 N 45th St.
Omaha, NE 68104
(402) 455-6262
www.Bigmamaskitchen.com

STELLANATOR
TIME

Hungry? Hungry enough to devour six burger patties, twelve pieces of bacon, six slices of cheese, and six fried eggs between a bun? Let's add lettuce, tomato, fried onions, jalapeño, peanut butter, and pickles. Add a side of French Fries and you get Stella's Stellanator challenge. It's free if you eat it all within forty-five minutes. You also get a T-shirt, plus your picture goes up on a wall of fame.Hundreds take on the challenge, but few win. For those not wide-eyed for a challenge, a regular burger will suffice. An Omaha favorite since 1936, Stella's offers interesting combinations on its burgers. Try one with bacon and peanut butter . . . or topped with a fried egg. The options offer an opportunity to create a tasty greasy spoon treat. Also, forget plates and silverware. Lay napkins on the table and get your fingers messy eating some of the best burgers you will ever taste.

106 Galvin Rd S
Bellevue, NE 68005
(402) 291-6088
www.Stellasbarandgrill.com

FUN FACT

Molly Schuyler set the record twice for eating a Stellanator. She first devoured the massive burger and fries in 6 minutes and 28 seconds and followed it with a showing of 3 minutes and 40 seconds. That record still stands. Schuyler became a professional competitive eater.

COFFEE
BREAK

You don't need to travel to Seattle for a great cup of joe. About a dozen local coffee shops call Omaha home. While some, such as Bellevue-based Scooters Coffee, offer the basics of a hot cup of coffee in a comfortable environment, others serve their java with a theme. Hardy Coffee combines coffee with a bakery, providing not only a flavorful fragrance but also a delicious visit. Hardy Coffee encourages visitors to make themselves at home during their visit, working on laptops, visiting with friends, or just relaxing. While Hardy Coffee's anchor location remains a stronghold of the Old Market area, the franchise has spread its wings by opening other locations around Omaha. The Omaha Bicycle Company, another unique coffee shop, resides in the Benson neighborhood. Visitors enjoy lattes and espressos while checking out the bicycle-infused décor, featuring actual bicycles dangling from the wall.

Hardy Coffee
1031 Jones St.
Omaha, NE 68102
(402) 934-7450
www.hardycoffee.com

Archetype Coffee
3926 Farnam St.
Omaha, NE 68131
www.drinkarchetype.com

Accelerando Coffee House
7023 Cass St.
Omaha, NE 68132
(402) 972-777

Culprit Cafe
1603 Farnam St., Ste 101
Omaha, NE 68102
www.culpritcafe.com

Omaha Bicycle Co.
6015 Maple St.
Omaha, NE 68104
(402) 315-9900
www.omahabicycleco.com

**The Bike Union/
The Coffee Union**
1818 Dodge St.
Omaha, NE 68102
(402) 345-0213
www.thebikeunion.org/
coffeehouse

Urban Abbey
1026 Jackson St.
Omaha, NE 68102
(402) 898-7600
www.urbanabbey.com

Scooter's
6303 Center St. #101
Omaha, NE 68106
(402) 504-3211
www.scooterscoffee.com

Roast Coffeehouse
1904 S 67th St.
Omaha, NE 68106
(402) 991-2326
www.ahillofbeans.com

EAT A MEAL
IN A POCKET

Everyone should taste the unique delicacy that is Runza. The Runza sandwich ranks at the top of Omaha's fast-food chain. A Runza consists of deliciously seasoned ground beef, mixed with cabbage and onions, baked inside a dough pocket. The Eastern European pierogi provided the inspiration for the Runza. Founded in 1949 in Lincoln, the family-owned restaurant expanded to other locations across Nebraska, including Omaha, as well as a few locations outside the state. When people move from Omaha, Runza always remains at the top of their to-eat lists when they return home. They drool for the freshly prepared sandwiches, burgers, and chicken. Add a side of crinkle-cut french fries or frings (a mix of fries and onion rings) and you're set. When cold weather strikes, the eatery also offers another Midwestern tradition—homemade chili and cinnamon rolls.

Several locations throughout Omaha
www.runza.com

FUN FACT
Runzas are served at Memorial Stadium in Lincoln during Nebraska Cornhuskers football games.

TRY LUNCH
ON FOUR WHEELS

Who doesn't enjoy grabbing a hot dog from a vendor's cart? How about some jambalaya or étouffé? Maybe you're a barbecue fan. Whatever your preference, chances are an Omaha food truck has it. The food truck industry has exploded around the city in recent years. In the old days, the Localmotive food truck dominated the scene, but today more than a dozen food trucks roam the city's streets, offering restaurant-quality entrees. From Taste of New Orleans' Cajun to the Dire Lion's British fish and chips, almost nothing is off the menu. The growth in popularity of food trucks led to a weekly downtown roundup where trucks park and people line up for a delicious lunch. Entertainment districts then added monthly food truck rodeos, which attract hundreds of people to the area.

Anthony Piccolo's Mobile Venue
anthonypiccolos.com/food-truck

Taste of New Orleans
www.facebook.com/A-Taste-of-New-Orleans-
279650875475653

Dire Lion
www.direlion.com

Mosaic Pickle
www.mosaicpickle.com

Maria Bonita
www.mariabonitaonline.com/food-trucks.html

For the Love of Food Truck
www.facebook.com/bestfoodtruckinbellevue

LeBlanc's BBQ Cajun and More
www.leblancsbbqandcajun.com

Scotty's Go-Go-Grill
www.facebook.com/Scotty's Go-Go-Grill

Only in NE experience

EAT WITH
THE RACCOONS

How many times have you seen a raccoon and thought, "Hey, I'd like to have dinner with that raccoon?" Well, at the Alpine Inn, you can . . . sort of. The northeast Omaha establishment offers diners a view of raccoons and feral cats sharing a dinner of leftovers on a patio. The owners unwittingly created the tradition in the 1970s after raccoons started showing up to eat scraps. Today, visitors actually seek the choice seats in the house, which are next to large viewing windows, where they can eat their fried chicken while watching the raccoons and cats feast on chicken, french fries, and other wild animal goodies. The Alpine Inn's fried chicken is a must and worth the 15–20 minute wait for it to be prepared, as it turns out perfectly cooked with the right amount of crunch and juices.

10405 Calhoun Rd.
Omaha, NE 68112
(402) 451-9988

TIP
Get there close to sunset for the best viewing of the raccoons' feast.

BIRTHPLACE
OF THE REUBEN

A late-night poker game at an Omaha hotel led to the creation of one of the most delicious and famous sandwiches in the world. A group of wealthy travelers staying at the former Blackstone Hotel—once the premier hotel between Chicago and San Francisco—were deeply involved in a card game when Reuben Kulakofsky allegedly summoned a hotel employee to have the chef make him a sandwich. Kulakofsky wanted something different, as he'd grown tired of the menu. In an attempt to please his guest, the chef tossed corned beef, cheese, and sauerkraut on bread and served it to the gambler. Thus, the Reuben was born, right here in River City. To relive history, grab Omaha's favorite Reuben at the Crescent Moon, which is located across the street from the Blackstone.

3578 Farnam St.
Omaha, NE 68131
(402)345-1708
www.beercornerusa.com/crescentmoon

ENJOY A TASTY
EUROPEAN TREAT

You know it's a close-knit community when a bakery identifies a people, and that's exactly why the Lithuanian Bakery is more than just a place to get bread. Opened in 1962, the South Omaha bakery helps tell the story of Lithuanian immigrants who settled here. The neighborhood served as the melting pot of Omaha during the late 1800s. Immigrants from several Eastern European countries sought freedom and a new life in the United States, with about four hundred Lithuanians among them. Today, people rush to the Lithuanian Bakery every Saturday morning in hopes of getting one of its famous tortes. Created over three days, this masterpiece features eight layers of wafers, each coated with vanilla buttercream and lemon extract, with a layer of apricot in the middle.

5217 South 33rd Ave.
Omaha, NE 68107
800-798-5217
www.lithuanianbakery.biz

HOW DO YOU LIKE
YOUR STEAK?

Rare. Medium rare. Well done. Regardless of how you like your steak, you'll find the perfect steakhouse in Omaha. Steakhouses have been around Omaha for decades, dating back to the days of the city's stockyards. Once the largest in the world, the stockyards led to the opening of dozens of steakhouses. With the growth of the yards, Johnny's Café—Omaha's oldest steakhouse at ninety-five years—converted from a saloon to a steakhouse to feed the farmers bringing animals to the stockyards. A visit to a steakhouse was once considered an event, so people would dress in suits and nice dresses to dine out. As the stockyards went away, Omaha's steak scene changed. Gone were the days of treating a trip to a steakhouse as an event. Today, Omaha remains a steakhouse stronghold on a new landscape, with contemporary restaurants challenging the classic eateries.

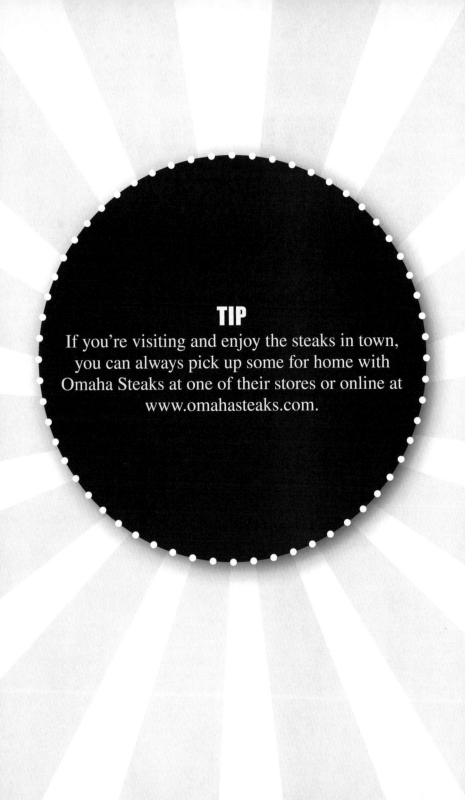

TIP

If you're visiting and enjoy the steaks in town, you can always pick up some for home with Omaha Steaks at one of their stores or online at www.omahasteaks.com.

Gorat's
4917 Center St., Omaha, NE 68106
(402) 551-3733
www.goratsomaha.com

Anthony's Steakhouse
7220 F St., Omaha, NE 68127
(402) 331-7575
www.anthonyssteakhouse.com

Cascio's Steakhouse
1620 S 10th St., Omaha, NE 68108
(402) 345-8313
www.casciossteakhouse.com

Johnny's Cafe
4702 S 27th St., Omaha, NE 68107
(402) 731-4774
www.johnnyscafe.com

Drover
2121 S 73rd St., Omaha, NE 68124
(402) 391-7440
www.droverrestaurant.com

Brother Sebastian's
1350 S 119th St., Omaha, NE 68144
(402) 330-0300
www.brothersebastians.com

Farmer Brown's
2620 River Road Dr., Waterloo, NE 68069
(402) 779-2353
www.farmerbrowns.com

ICE CREAM WORTH
STANDING IN LINE FOR

You know that when people are willing to stand outside in line for thirty to forty-five minutes for an ice cream treat, that particular ice cream must be the best around. As for Ted and Wally's in the Old Market, that description is spot on. Opened in 1984 in a former car repair shop, Ted and Wally's attracts fans for their more than two thousand flavors of homemade ice cream, including vanilla bean, Dutch chocolate, and lime butternut squash. The catch is that you never know which flavors will be on the menu, as it changes daily. The Ted and Wally's team creates delicious, creamy frozen treats by combining 18 percent real butterfat with eggs. The ice cream is created on-site in 20-gallon containers surrounded by rock salt and ice. Once ready to be served, customers enjoy ice cream in cones, sundaes, or shakes.

1120 Jackson St.
Omaha, NE 68102
(402) 341-5827
www.tedandwallys.com

TRY A SLICE
OF LITTLE ITALY

Nearly a century after opening, Orsi's Bakery remains a stalwart in Omaha's Little Italy neighborhood. Its handmade Sicilian-style pizza ranks among the city's most popular pizzas. A few blocks from the Missouri River, Orsi's attracts people from as far away as west Omaha. Its menu also offers goudarooni, which is a double-crusted pizza. Plan your pizza to go, as Orsi's has limited seating space. Beyond its dynamite pizza and bread, the bakery features Italian cooking supplies and a small deli. Walking inside, you immediately notice the framed pictures, which serve as a photographic sports hall of fame, featuring athletes ranging from local wrestling to pro football. A destructive fire in the late 1990s solidified Orsi's role as the center of Little Italy when neighbors held fund-raisers to help rebuild it.

Orsi's Italian Bakery and Pizzeria
621 Pacific St.
Omaha, NE 68108
(402) 345-3438
www.orsibakery.com

Other places to grab a slice

Lighthouse Pizza
1004 S 74th Plz.
Omaha, NE 68114
(402) 932-6660
www.lhpizza.com

Big Fred's Pizza
1101 S 119th St.
Omaha, NE 68144
(402) 333-4414
www.bigfreds.pizza

Zio's Pizzeria
3 locations
www.zios-pizzeria.com

Dante Ristorante Pizzeria
2 locations
www.dantepizzeria.com

Don Carmelo's
2 locations
www.doncarmelos.com

Mama's Pizza
3 locations
www.mamaspizzaomaha.com

Ragazzi's
2 locations
www.ragazzi-pizza.com

BREW
TIME

As you swallow that perfectly chilled brew, rest easy knowing that Omaha knows its beer. The city's beer history dates to the 1860s when Metz opened the first brewery in Nebraska. Krug and Storz joined soon after to give Omaha a strong German-influenced beer. Storz was the only brewery to survive Prohibition and stayed in business through 1972. Today, Omaha enjoys a solid craft beer scene, with about a dozen breweries calling the area home. Nebraska Brewing Company and Lucky Bucket likely rate as the best known of the crop. The breweries are small businesses in action, operating with skeleton crews, while canning and bottling their brews by hand. Nebraska Brewing churns out about ninety barrels of beer a day, while Lucky Bucket produces about twenty barrels.

Lucky Bucket Brewery
11941 Centennial Rd.
La Vista, NE 68128
(402) 763-8868
www.luckybucketbrewing.com

Nebraska Brewing Company
7474 Towne Center Pkwy. Ste. 101
Papillion, NE 68046
(402) 934-7100
www.nebraskabrewingco.com

Upstream Brewery
514 S 11th St.
Omaha, NE 68102
(402) 344-0200
www.upstreambrewing.com

Farnam House Brewing Company
3558 Farnam St.
Omaha, NE 68131
(402) 401-6086
www.farnamhousebrewing.com

Brickway Brewing and Distillery
1116 Jackson St.
Omaha, NE 68102
(402) 933-2613
http://www.drinkbrickway.com

The Benson Brewery
6059 Maple St.
Omaha, NE 68104
(402) 934-8668
www.bensonbrewery.com

Kros Strain Brewrey
Portal Plaza Business Park
Building C
10411 Portal Rd. Ste. 102
La Vista, NE 68128
(402) 779-7990
www.krosstrainbrewing.com

Infusion Brewing Company
6115 Maple St.
Omaha, NE 68104
(402) 916-9998
www.infusionbrewing.com

Jaipur Brewing Company
10922 Elm St.
Omaha, NE 68144
(402) 392-7331
www.jaipurindianfood.com

Scriptown Brewing Company
3922 Farnam St.
Omaha, NE 68131
(402) 991-0506
www.scriptownbrewing.com

RELAX WITH
A GLASS

Enjoy a glass of wine, perhaps a sweet Edelweiss, kick back, and take in the soft sounds of the artist performing on stage at Soaring Wings Vineyard & Brewing. Weekly concerts highlight a visit to the Sarpy County winery. Soaring Wings started growing a variety of grapes in 2001 and served their first wines three years later. Today, the winery remains a popular attraction, drawing people in for its special events, such as the annual balloon festival. During its fall festival, you can stomp grapes as part of the fun. In 2011, the winery expanded its résumé by adding a microbrewery. Now serving nine beers with its award-winning twenty wines, Soaring Wings continues to grow and provide guests opportunities to expand their taste horizons.

17111 S 138th St.
Springfield, NE 68059
(402) 253-2479
www.soaringwingswine.com

FARM
TO TABLE

The Grey Plume separates itself from other restaurants in Omaha with its farm-to-table menu, a concept that immediately caught on with locals when it opened in 2010. Owner/chef Clayton Chapman works with twenty regional farms and distributors on daily deliveries to ensure the evening's menu features fresh and local ingredients. The staff even churns butter on-site. The Grey Plume's menu often changes based on items' availability. Chapman has been nominated many times for the exalted James Beard Award as a top chef in the country. His commitment to sustainability includes using green energy to control the temperature in the restaurant as well as recycled wood, including barn wood for the flooring. The Grey Plume has been a featured partner of Midtown Crossing since the retail district opened.

220 S 31st Ave., Ste. 3101
Omaha, NE 68131
(402) 763-4447
www.thegreyplume.com

AS SEEN
ON TV

Omaha's reputation as a foodie town has grown over the years. From thick, juicy, mouthwatering steaks to sweet cupcakes, about twenty eateries have been featured on national television shows. Food Network's *Diners, Drive-Ins and Dives* visited about six restaurants, including California Tacos and More. The midtown Omaha restaurant features the California Taco, a large fried softshell taco with all the fixins. The taco attracts college students and business executives alike and is actually a meal in itself. Open since the 1930s, Joe Tess Place's reputation as the THE place to eat fresh fish remains strong. Once you taste the catfish, you'd swear it was pulled fresh from the Missouri River. Following a great meal, nothing beats dessert at Jones Bros. Cupcakes at Aksarben Village, which was featured on *Cupcake Wars*.

eCreamery
5001 Underwood Ave.
Omaha, NE 68132
(402) 934-3888
www.ecreamery.com

California Tacos and More
3235 California St.
Omaha, NE 68131
(402) 342-0212
www.californiatacosandmore.com

Over Easy
13859 Q St.
Omaha, NE 68135
(402) 934-2929
www.overeasy.com

Amato's
6405 Center St.
Omaha, NE 68106
(402) 558-5010

Jones Bros. Cupcakes
2121 S 67th St.
Omaha, NE 68106
www.jonesbroscupcakes.com

The Drover
2121 S 73rd St.
Omaha, NE
(402) 391-7440
www.droverrestaurant.com

Joe Tess Place
5424 S 24th St.
Omaha, NE 68107
(402) 731-7278
www.joetessplace.com

BREAKFAST
AT LISA'S

Whether you sit at the counter, a table, or a booth, at Lisa's Radial Cafe, you'll become friends with the strangers sitting next to you, striking up a conversation about this uniquely decorated eatery. Lisa, the owner, loved Lucille Ball, and the restaurant reflects it with *I Love Lucy* memorabilia scattered about the cafe. The cafe also has one wall dedicated to the works of local artists. Located near St. Cecilia Cathedral, it's more than just a neighborhood eatery. People can spend up to an hour in line, anticipating Lisa's delicious entrees, such as the Radial Raft, which features two eggs, biscuits, and hash browns in a sea of gravy. You can also enjoy omelets or skillets. The breakfast menu is the most popular, but Lisa's does offer lunch daily except Sunday.

817 N 40th St.
Omaha, NE 68131
(402) 551-2176
www.facebook.com/lisasradialcafe

WHO NEEDS
NEW YORK?

With every bite of your succulent duck or your juicy T-bone steak at the Flatiron Cafe, you enjoy a morsel of Omaha history. Calling the Flatiron building home since 1995, the Flatiron Cafe experience also offers you a chance to enjoy century-old architecture and an impressive view of Omaha's skyscrapers. Built in the early 1900s, the Flatiron resembled its famous cousin in New York, with its three sides situated on a triangular corner. Originally used to house offices and apartments, Omaha's Flatiron soon converted to a hotel. Mobsters reportedly called the Hotel Flatiron home during the city's organized crime heyday. The Georgian Revival–style building converted to office space during the 1970s before reverting to its original use in 2015.

1722 St. Mary's Ave. #110
Omaha, NE 68102
(402) 344-3040
www.theflatironcafe.com

A GOOD MEAL
FOR A GOOD CAUSE

Who doesn't enjoy eating for a good cause? In Omaha, hundreds of people dine out over a 10-day period known as "Restaurant Week." More than fifty restaurants participate as a fund-raiser for a local food bank. Restaurants offer preset three-course menus for prices ranging from $20 to $50. Diners can choose from casual eateries to upscale restaurants, so you can have a burger or maybe a fancy duck dish. It's your choice based on the available options. Restaurant Week restaurants donate a portion of their proceeds to the food bank to help people who may need assistance. Restaurant Week started in 2011 when local chefs created the event as a platform to showcase their menus and attract new diners and fans.

www.visitomaha.com/restaurantweek

CHAMPAGNE ON TAP?
YES, PLEASE

Order a glass of champagne from the tap, grab a table, and check out the vintage news on the walls during a visit to the Homy Inn. Champagne on tap? The original owner thought it would be a fun way to attract patrons. The Homy Inn offers four types of champagne, which can also be served in a pitcher. Opened in 1956 and originally named the Homey Inn, the owners shortened it when they realized not all the letters would fit on the sign. Named as a top 50 U.S. bar by *Esquire,* the family-owned business became an Omaha icon over the years, known as a dive bar where everyone wants to stop in for a drink. The bar embraces an eclectic décor with Beatles memorabilia as well as plates, pins, and menus tacked to the ceiling.

1510 N Saddle Creek Rd.
Omaha, NE 68104
(402) 554-5815
www.homyinn.com

Should experience
Can order Italian from across the street

OMAHA
ORIGINALS

Next time you heat up a frozen meal in a microwave, you can thank Omaha. Many delicious inventions have been created here over the years. Frozen meals took off after Swanson's invented the TV dinner in the early 1950s at its downtown plant. An Omaha "original," Little King opened its first sandwich shop in 1969, expanding nationwide to more than a hundred stores in seventeen states. While Little King didn't last as a national chain, it remains a favorite local brand, led by its well-loved Royal Treat sub. Starting with a small pizza shop in Omaha, Willie Thiesen grew Godfather's Pizza into a popular national chain. Eventually selling the company to a major food company, Thiesen continues to dabble in the food industry. America's "Best Philly" calls Omaha home. Created in 2002, Pepperjax combines the best of Philadelphia hoagies with Midwestern meats to create a tasty Philly sandwich.

TIP
Butter Brickle ice cream was invented in Omaha. Today, find the best home-made Butter Brickle at Coneflower Creamery in the Blackstone District.

3921 Farnam St.
Omaha, NE 68131
(402) 913-2399
coneflowercreamery.com

Pepperjax
several locations
www.pepperjaxgrill.com

Godfather's Pizza
www.godfathers.com

Little King
several locations
www.littlekingsubs.com

Orpheum

Omaha Performing Arts Presents

MILLION DOLLAR QUARTET

Feb 18-23

watchfire

Orph

MARTHA G
DANCE CO

Performing App

Ja

MUSIC AND ENTERTAINMENT

OLD-TIME MOVIE
HOUSE

Once the place to watch cult classics and foreign movies, the Dundee Theater fell on hard times. Opened in 1925 as a vaudeville theater, the Dundee soon changed its format to showing movies. As Omaha's lone single-screen theater, the Dundee often ran movies that weren't likely to show up at the multiscreen complexes. Midnight movies were popular with younger crowds; some would bring props to throw at the screen for such films as *The Rocky Horror Picture Show*. As time ravaged it, the Dundee's owners couldn't afford to maintain its upkeep. The theater closed for renovation and sat empty for a few years until Filmstreams took it over. The independent theater company sought to include the Dundee as a partner with its downtown location. Renovation plans included gutting the interior while maintaining its classic street front façade.

4952 Dodge St.
Omaha, NE 68132
(402) 558-0397
www.filmstreams.org

CHECK OUT AN ACT
AT THE LINK

The arena lights darken, and fans start to work up a frenzy. Then the spotlight shines on the stage, and fifteen thousand fans scream and applaud as the singer belts out the first words of a hit song. Welcome to concert night at the CenturyLink Center Omaha. The arena attracts major performers, including Paul McCartney, Bob Dylan, Lady Gaga, and Taylor Swift, but it is used for so much more than concerts. Omaha has hosted the U.S. Olympic swim trials since 2008. About eighteen thousand fans routinely attend Creighton University basketball games. Several companies, including Warren Buffett's Berkshire kick-started, host conventions here. Opened in 2003, the arena kick started the riverfront development that now includes one of the world's longest pedestrian bridges, a 1½-mile walking trail, condos, and offices as well as riverboat tours. Once opened, the CenturyLink Center replaced the aged Civic Auditorium.

455 N 10th St.
Omaha, NE 68102
www.centurylinkcenteromaha.com

BEAT
THE CLOCK

The door shuts behind you, and the clock starts counting down. You know you only have an hour to find and solve the clues to access the key that will open that door and win your challenge at the Locked Room. If you don't, you'll sink to the bottom of the sea with the Titanic. You scan the room. You scan your partners' faces. Scrambling to solve the first clue eventually leads to the next one and so on. While solving the clues challenges you, the event creates a fun night out at any of Omaha's themed escape room locations. Each one offers a variety of themes, so fans can enjoy playing many different games. By the way, the clock continues to count down.

Locked Room
741 N 120th St.
Omaha, NE 68154
(402) 504-3444
www.lockedroomomaha.com

The Escape Omaha
6315 Center St.
Omaha, NE 68106
(402) 506-6682
www.theescapeomaha.com

Entrap Games
7905 L St., Ste. 110
Omaha, NE 68127
(402) 991-9169
www.entrapgames.com

House of Conundrum
2564 Leavenworth St.
Omaha, NE 68105
(402) 250-2300
www.houseofconundrum.com

Get Out Omaha
501 S 13th St.
Omaha, NE 68102
(402) 915-1853
www.getoutomaha.com

Crack the Code
3457 S 84th St.
Omaha, NE 68124
(402) 391-6225
www.crackthecodeescaperooms.com

WELCOME TO
OMAHA'S BROADWAY

Broadway-quality performances own the stage today, but the Orpheum Theater once dominated the area with live vaudeville acts. Opened in 1927, the Orpheum rated as the place to be to watch live performances. As stage shows faded with movie theater popularity, the Orpheum changed with the times. The theater operated as a film house beginning in the early 1960s. Because of structural damage through the years, the Orpheum closed in 1971. Donated to the city, a local organization required the 2,500-seat theater to host only plays and musicals. Today, the Orpheum hosts some of the best Broadway touring shows. The stage features a trap door designed specifically for *Wicked,* which continues to be a popular musical in Omaha. The theater also stands out for its Italianate design, featuring original lobby chandeliers and drapes.

409 S 16th St.
Omaha, NE 68102
(402) 661-8501
www.omahaperformingarts.org

GET YOUR
GEEK ON

Where else can you dress as your favorite movie or comic character and hang out with like-minded friends? The Omaha area celebrates all things comics, movies, and pop culture with not just one but two pop culture conventions. O Comic Con primarily features American pop culture, while BritishFest focuses on steampunk and other action from across the pond. O Comic Con started in 2015 and is still growing; convention organizers are gaining a foothold with attracting well-known celebrities, such as *Star Trek's* Walter Koenig and *Guardians of the Galaxy's* Sean Gunn. BritishFest's guests often include actors from the *Doctor Who* series. While mingling with celebrities is fun, the best part of the conventions may be the costumes. Cosplayers of all ages bring their favorite characters to life—you can find yourself traveling through time and space with Doctor Who or Star-Lord or live out a fairy tale with Maleficent.

O Comic Con
www.ocomiccon.com

BritishFest
www.britishfest.weebly.com

ENJOY
FESTIVAL SEASON

Omaha's summer festival season runs the gamut from food to pirates, with more than fifty events packing the calendar. It seems that a festival or an event is happening around the metro area every weekend throughout summer. The festival season kicks off with Taste of Omaha the first weekend of June. The event attracts thousands to the riverfront area, with local food, vendors, and music stretching from the Heartland of America Park to the Bob Kerrey pedestrian bridge. If art is more your thing, then the Summer Arts Festival is a must the following weekend. The city closes off about six blocks from traffic downtown for the three-day event, which features nearly 150 regional artists. Near the end of the summer festivities, cosplay and giant turkey leg fans head to the Renaissance Faire or Pirate Festival at the Bellevue Berry Farm.

Summer Arts Festival
www.summerarts.org

Taste of Omaha
www.showofficeonline.com/TasteHome

Pirate Festival
www.bellevueberryfarm.com/pirate-festival

Renaissance Festival
www.bellevueberryfarm.com/renaissance-festival

WHERE
ART THOU?

"Good night, good night! Parting is such sweet sorrow, that I shall say good night til it be morrow." Clad in authentic medieval wardrobe, he speaks these words to his true love, as the audience watches in awe. Fans of William Shakespeare's *Romeo and Juliet* and other works by the British playwright enjoy taking in an outdoor production during "Shakespeare on the Green." The Nebraska Shakespeare troupe presents two Shakespeare plays each summer at Elmwood Park, near the campus of the University of Nebraska at Omaha. Fans lay blankets along the hillside, while others watch from their lawn chairs; some bring picnic baskets so that they can enjoy dinner and a show. In its fourth decade, "Shakespeare on the Green" helps Nebraska Shakespeare educate the public about the bard.

www.nebraskashakespeare.com

SMOOTH
TUNES

Music echoes off the buildings behind you, as bands play smooth tunes on a nearby stage. Lying on blankets over the lush green grass or sitting in lawn chairs, Omahans flock to Jazz on the Green at Turner Park each summer for a six-week series featuring some of the best jazz music in the country. Friends and families join together to share appetizers and drinks while enjoying the sounds from the stage. You'll hear both jazz and some blues tunes. The music series started at Joslyn Museum near downtown more than three decades ago but outgrew the venue and moved to Turner Park near Midtown Crossing in 2010, with crowds topping ten thousand at some shows.

30th and Farnam Sts.
Omaha, NE 68131
(402) 557-6006
www.midtowncrossing.com/events/jazz-on-the-green/

BANG
YOUR HEAD

Grab a few friends and check out your favorite band in an intimate setting. Omaha's music scene has grown since the early 1990s, with indie and major artists recording at local studios. Small venues scattered around the city offer bands opportunities to perform in small settings. A favorite spot for both national and regional acts to play is the Waiting Room in the Benson neighborhood. The 400-person capacity club provides a great setting for performers, such as Indigenous and Colin Hay, and their fans to interact in a cozy environment, where the audience is a mere few feet from the band. Omaha's best-known venue may be the Slowdown, which provides an impressive setting for mainly indie acts in front of a crowd of less than a thousand fans. The nearly century-old Sokol Auditorium hosts a variety of events, including concerts and professional wrestling.

Slowdown
729 N 14th St., Omaha, NE 68102
(402) 345-7569
www.theslowdown.com

Sokol Auditorium
2234 S 13th St., Omaha, NE 68108
(402) 346-9802
www.facebook.com/
sokolauditoriumandunderground

The Waiting Room Lounge
6212 Maple St., Omaha, NE 68104
(402) 884-5353
www.waitingroomlounge.com

CONCERT
IN A "SHOEBOX"

A shoebox hosting concerts? Opened in 2005, architects based the Holland Performing Arts Center's design on straight lines and angles, using glass walls to provide natural lighting. The "shoebox" concept allows for long and narrow concert halls, which offer outstanding acoustics. Seating two thousand people, the main venue features major concerts, including jazz and contemporary artists as well as symphony and opera productions. The Holland hosts a classic movie screening with the symphony providing live musical accompaniment. The facility features two additional concert venues. A smaller concert hall seats about five hundred people and provides an intimate setting for performances, while a courtyard allows for outdoor shows. When it opened, the Holland Performing Arts Center served as an overflow theater for the older Orpheum Theater but grew into a major venue itself.

1200 Douglas St.
Omaha, NE 68102
(402) 345-0202
www.omahaperformingarts.org

ACT LIKE
A KID

At Omaha's Rose Theater, kids catch the acting bug on the big stage in front of hundreds of fans. The children's theater presents professional-quality productions several times a year, with rotating casts. Originally the Emmy Gifford Children's Theater, the company moved downtown to the former Astro movie theater when Rose Blumkin, founder of Nebraska Furniture Mart, bought the classic building in the 1980s. Fortunately, she prevented the building from being demolished. Opened in 1927 using Moorish architecture, its interior includes a courtyard design featuring fountains. Renamed in honor of Blumkin, the Rose's theater company encourages children's interests in theater arts through acting or stage production work. The Rose was also recognized as one of the top 20 children's theaters in the country by *USA Today*.

2001 Farnam St.
Omaha, NE 68102
(402) 345-4849
www.rosetheater.org

LIGHT UP
THE SEASON

More than a million white lights shine during Omaha's Holiday Lights Festival. The annual event kicks off Thanksgiving night as the mayor flips the switch to light about forty blocks downtown, beginning at the Gene Leahy Pedestrian Mall. The lights festival, which lasts through New Year's Day, features carolers around the Old Market on weekends and concerts at the Holland Performing Arts Center. Children visit with Santa Claus at the Durham Museum, while parents sip hot chocolate. Downtown museums and attractions also offer free admission during the Family Festival weekend. Aspiring Olympians practice their triple axel, while others work to stay upright on the Capitol District's ice rink. As the Holiday Lights Festival comes to an end, fireworks light up the sky New Year's Eve.

www.holidaylightsfestival.org

LEGENDS
ON THE STAGE

Henry Fonda launched his acting career at the Omaha Community Playhouse. Encouraged to act in a play by none other than Marlon Brando's mother, the future Academy Award winner first acted in The *King and I*. Fonda went on to break into movies and enjoyed roles in such hits as *The Grapes of Wrath and On Golden Pond*. Meanwhile, the Omaha Community Playhouse moved locations, settling in at its current site in 1956. It's the nation's largest community playhouse and houses two stages. The Howard and Rhonda Hawks Mainstage Theatre seats 558 people, home to the theater's annual Christmas Carol production. The Howard Drew Theater (which presents plays in the Fonda-McGuire series) seats about two hundred people for the Playhouse's progressive shows. In addition to Fonda's success, Omaha native and movie star Dorothy McGuire started her acting career here at the age of thirteen.

6915 Cass St., Omaha, NE 68132
402-553-0800
www.omahaplayhouse.com

Actors who have called Omaha home:

Swoosie Kurtz	Gabrielle Union	Jay Karnes
Andrew Rannells	Anne Ramsey	John Beasley
Adam Devine	David Doyle	Nick Nolte
Lori Petty	Inga Swenson	

SPORTS AND RECREATION

CROWN A
CHAMPION

From that first pitch at the old Johnny Rosenblatt Stadium in June 1950, a love affair grew between college baseball and Omaha. Today, teams set their sights on the College World Series at TD Ameritrade Park on "The Road to Omaha." Eight teams compete to win the NCAA baseball championship in a double-elimination format. To get fans psyched up for the games, the CWS introduces teams in an Olympic-style opening. Teams enter the field carrying their school's flag as fans cheer them on. Afterward, a concert features a nationally known act, such as O.A.R. or Aloe Blacc. The nightcap includes a fireworks show. While teams come to win a title, fans from around the country flock to Omaha for more. Besides the action, fans participate in events surrounding the stadium, such as concerts, parties, and Fan Fest, featuring interactive exhibits and eating challenges. In the end, though, the games dominate, and fans fill the stadium, averaging about twenty-three thousand per game.

1200 Mike Fahey St.
Omaha, NE 68102
www.cwsomaha.com

FUN FACT
University of Nebraska and Creighton University
have both appeared in the CWS.

FLY LIKE A
BLUEJAY

The action before the game rivals the action on the court at a Creighton University men's basketball game. The school ranks among the nation's best in game attendance, regularly appearing in the top 15, with a packed house of more than seventeen thousand fans to cheer the Bluejays on to victory. Before the team takes the court, fans stir themselves into a frenzy, and it begins with the student section. The "Blue Crew" features fans wearing blue and white pinstriped overalls, jumping to music blaring from arena speakers. As the players are introduced and ready to play, students unleash one last cheer and throw newspaper confetti into the air. With its talent and hometown support, Creighton is nearly unbeatable on its home court, annually challenging for conference championships. Creighton's success usually ends in postseason action, appearing in eighteen postseason tournaments in the past two decades, including eleven trips to the NCAA tourney.

Creighton University Basketball
CenturyLink Center
www.gocreighton.com/schedule.aspx?path=mbb

COME ON IN,
THE WATER'S FINE

At Diventures, they want you to believe in adventure. Opened in 2009, the diving and swim center encourages students to maximize their talent and skills whether it's scuba diving certification or swimming. Diventures offers twelve to thirty-six diving trips each year, ranging from local sites to international destinations, such as Fiji and Cozumel. While scuba lessons are a large part of the operation, three hundred to seven hundred people also take weekly swimming and kayak classes. Even with the high demand, Diventures maintains a small student-to-teacher ratio to ensure students receive personal instruction. Swim students even have the opportunity to take mermaid and shark classes, wearing fin bodysuits. The center offers additional classes, including aquatic Zumba and low-impact arthritis treatment. Founded in Omaha, Diventures has expanded to include six locations around the Midwest.

4303 W 121st Plaza
Omaha, NE 68137
(402) 933-6251
www.diventures.com

RUN THE
STAIRS

At the First National Bank Tower, people line up for a chance to reach the top of the building in only a few minutes. "Trek the Tower" encourages people of all ages and fitness levels to climb forty floors to reach the finish line after 633 feet. Working with Welcom, an organization that seeks to improve workplace wellness, the fund-raiser attracts nearly two thousand participants every February. Winners typically finish the 870-step ascent in about five minutes, while the average completion time is about twelve to fifteen minutes. Firefighters typically run the race while wearing their full gear. Opened in 2002, with forty-five stories, the First National Bank Tower tops Omaha's skyline as the tallest building. It replaced the 30-story Woodmen of the World building as Omaha's tallest.

1601 Dodge St.
Omaha, NE 68197
(402) 934-5795
www.trekupthetower.org

GOLF
WITH DINO

Line up your putt, aim around the 20-foot long T-Rex, but make sure the Brontosaurus doesn't swallow the ball before it hits the hole. At Prehistoric Putt, lifelike dinosaur figures hug the Jurassic-style miniature golf course. Opened in early 2017, Prehistoric Putt offers golfers two 18-hole courses to play, with unique challenges including holes featuring foosball, volcano, and plinko obstacles. If golfing with dinosaurs isn't on your bucket list, perhaps you can grab a parrot and head to Pirate Putt, Prehistoric Putt's sister course in nearby Council Bluffs. Here you can walk the plank aboard a pirate ship or hang out with pirate figures along the course, while facing such obstacles as warped walls, plinko, and a spring-loaded cannon that shoots your ball toward the hole.

Prehistoric Putt
11134 Q St.
Omaha, NE 68137
(402) 506-5204
www.letsgoputt.com

Pirate Putt
1718 Madison Ave.
Council Bluffs, IA 51503
(712) 355-8525
www.letsgoputt.com

PLAY
BALL!

When you hear the crack of the bat at Werner Park, you know you're in for some exciting baseball. The stadium is home to the Omaha Storm Chasers, the top farm club for Major League Baseball's Kansas City Royals. The Royals' World Series championships included homegrown talent they developed through their farm system, including the team in Omaha. The relationship between the two clubs has spanned five decades, as Omaha has been the only Triple-A team in Royals' history. Known as the Omaha Royals for almost forty-five years, the team changed its name to Storm Chasers when it moved to a new 9,000-seat ballpark in suburban Papillion in 2011. While mom or dad watch the game, children can play at the family fun zone, which features inflatables and a merry go-round.

12356 Ballpark Way
Papillion, NE 68046
(402) 738-5100
www.omahastormchasers.com

FUN FACT
The Storm Chasers won their division title
(including two Triple-A national championships)
the first four seasons they played at Werner Park.

SHOOT
AND SCORE

Omaha, where children dream of growing up to play their favorite sport . . . hockey? Indeed, Omaha enjoys a core of hockey fans who support programs from peewee to college. The University of Nebraska-Omaha provides some exciting action on the ice. In its third decade of playing Division I hockey, Omaha takes on some of the toughest teams in the game, such as national champions North Dakota, Denver, and Minnesota-Duluth to name a few in the National Collegiate Hockey Conference. To help navigate its growth, Omaha hired coaching legend Dean Blais. As a result, Omaha challenged for the national title in the 2014–15 season, reaching the NCAA Frozen Four tournament. Omaha has experienced nine winning seasons, and has played in the national playoffs three times. Omaha has sent eleven players to the National Hockey League, including the first two in program history to win the Stanley Cup, Jake Guentzel and Josh Archibald.

Baxter Arena—Home of UNO Hockey
2425 S 67th St.
Omaha, NE 68106
(402) 554-6200
www.omavs.com

HIT A HOME RUN
AT THE JOHNNY

Johnny Rosenblatt Stadium, known as the "ballpark on the hill" because it was the first thing visitors saw as they traveled into Omaha from Iowa, provided excitement for baseball fans for sixty years. Home to the College World Series and the minor league Omaha Royals, fans watched some of the best baseball in the country from 1950 to 2010. As Rosenblatt faded, Omaha built a downtown stadium near the riverfront. When Rosenblatt was demolished to allow for expansion at the nearby Henry Doorly Zoo, officials kept the infield intact, allowing its memory to live on. Rosenblatt fans still bring their children to have them stand at home plate and relive its history or play a pickup game, with the old Rosenblatt sign standing above left field.

Infield at the Zoo
3701 S 10th St.
Omaha, NE 68107
(402) 733-8401
www.omahazoo.com

CRUISIN'
THE PLATTE

It's been said the Platte River in Nebraska is "a mile wide and an inch deep." How do you boat on a river that's only a few inches deep? Enter Bryson's Airboat Tours. Bryson's offers airboat tours along the river near Fremont, about thirty minutes outside Omaha. Started in 2004 as a private boat ride, Bryson's quickly gained popularity, and today tours fill up fast. With a jet-style propeller and powered by an aircraft engine, the boat's loudness fades into the background as riders observe the natural beauty hugging the shoreline. Bluffs and trees combine to create postcard scenes, and the pilot maneuvers the boat around sandbars just below the water's surface. Make it an event while onshore by grilling and playing games, such as horseshoes.

879 Co. Rd. 19
Fremont, NE 68025
(402) 968-8534
www.brysonsairboattours.com

ZIP ON
DOWN

Your experience begins with a ride up the ski lift, giving you time to think about what's to come. As you climb the tower at the Mount Crescent Zipline nearing the platform from where you'll launch, feelings of exhilaration and excitement creep in. Once the harness is attached to the zipline, you give a thumb's up signal and away you go, speeding downhill over 1,600 feet traveling at 40 mph. The longest outdoor zipline in the Midwest offers dual racing with side-by-side ziplines. Once the weather starts to cool and the zipline season ends, Mount Crescent transitions into downhill skiing. With snowmaking equipment that rivals the machines at the Rocky Mountain resorts, every day is a ski day during winter.

17026 Snowhill Ln.
Honey Creek, IA 51542
(712) 545-3850
www.skicrescent.com

AND THEY'RE
OFF!

Watching the ponies run at Aksarben (Nebraska spelled backwards) once dominated the Omaha sports scene. Trainers from around the country brought their best thoroughbreds to town for a chance to win races. When other forms of gaming came along—casinos and keno—attendance dropped, and the race track closed in 1995. In the end, a great race and arena complex was demolished for retail and office space. Even so, horse racing fans longed to keep the sport alive in Omaha. So, in 1998, Horsemen's Park opened, initially offering simulcast racing, but soon the park offered live horse racing, eventually expanding to three racing weekends a year. More than three thousand fans pack the bleachers to watch their favorite horse come around the corner and leg out the final stretch.

6303 Q St.
Omaha, NE 68117
(402) 731-2900
www.horsemenspark.com

FUN FACT
Triple Crown winner Omaha was buried near the old Aksarben racetrack. A memorial in his honor is located at Stinson Park at Aksarben Village retail center.

WATCH INDOOR
FOOTBALL'S OLDEST TEAM

Nebraska is known for being the home of University of Nebraska Cornhuskers football. What goes with corn? In Omaha, fans would say the Beef . . . as in the Omaha Beef. The nation's longest running indoor football team competes in the Champions Indoor Football League. The Beef provides a fun experience at the "Slaughterhouse," fans' nickname for the 4,000-seat Ralston Arena. The team has fourteen playoff appearances, including three as division champions. The Beef came up short in its two league championship games. The Beef entertains its fans with its cheerleading group, the Prime Dancers, while the Rump Roasters, a group of girthy men, perform a dance during halftime. The Beef made national news when it offered former Heisman Trophy winner Tim Tebow a $75 per game contract after he was cut by his last NFL team.

7300 Q St.
Ralston, NE 68108
(402) 346-2333
www.beeffootball.com

TALK WITH
THE ANIMALS

It's easy to see why the Henry Doorly Zoo and Aquarium routinely ranks as one of the best zoos in the world, even topping some charts. With the indoor Desert Dome leading the way, the zoo is home to some of the largest indoor exhibits in the world, including the Kingdoms of the Night's swamp and the Lied Jungle Rainforest. Bring your walking shoes to explore the zoo's seventeen major attractions, or view exhibits by train or from above on the Skyfari lift ride. The Henry Doorly Zoo continually seeks to expand and offer new attractions for visitors. Between 2016 and 2017, the zoo added its African Grasslands with its elephants and giraffes, Alaskan Adventure splash area, Birds of Flight Program, and Children's Adventure Trail interactive exhibit.

3701 S 10th St.
Omaha, NE 68107
(402) 733-8401
www.omahazoo.com

FUN FACT
The Omaha zoo has been actively involved with conservation efforts in Madagascar since 1998.

GO ON
A SAFARI

As you pass through the gate, you see elk roaming near the top of a hill or cooling off from the summer heat in their water hole. Once you see the elk, you'll enjoy the four-mile drive through the Lee G. Simmons Conservation Park and Wildlife Safari, located about twenty minutes west of Omaha. Opened in 1998 as a sister attraction to the Omaha Zoo, the wildlife park provides an up-close viewing experience. Catch a herd of roaming bison, pelicans in the wetlands, and Sandhill Cranes and other birds in Crane Meadows. The park features a walking area where you can visit Wolf Canyon, catching glimpses of grey wolves or black bears. Children can also interact with pygmy goats and chickens at the Hands-on Corral.

16406 292nd St.
Ashland, NE 68003
(402) 944-9453
www.wildlifesafaripark.com

STROLL ON
THE MIGHTY MO

Cruise along the river, cross the nation's longest pedestrian bridge, or sit back and take in the sights and sounds along Omaha's riverfront. Bordered by the Missouri River, Omaha's riverfront offers a plethora of attractions, such as a mile-and-a-half long trail for walking or bicycling, or learning about the Lewis and Clark expedition at the National Park Service headquarters building. As you stroll along the trail, check out Omaha's labor union history with the "Salute to Labor" monument, which is the country's second-largest labor memorial. You can also enjoy life on the river with a cruise on the River City Star paddleboat, which highlights the city's skyline among other attractions. Or you can walk the Bob Kerrey pedestrian bridge as it crosses the Missouri River, connecting Nebraska and Iowa.

Lewis and Clark Historic Trail Headquarters and Visitors Center
601 Riverfront Dr.
Omaha, NE 68102
(402) 661-1804
www.nps.gov/lecl/planyourvisit/leclvchq2b.htm

BE IN TWO STATES
AT ONE TIME

Locals and visitors love the Bob Kerrey pedestrian bridge. Named in honor of a former Nebraska senator and governor, the Kerrey Bridge, affectionately known as "Bob," shines as an icon for Omaha. People use the mile-and-a-half long bridge for recreation, including walking, bicycling, and running, with the city's skyline beaming in the background. Connecting Nebraska and Iowa, people pose for photos at the state line midway across the Missouri River. The Iowa side entertains people with an amphitheater and playground. At the Omaha base of the bridge, a dancing fountain and picnic area create summer fun for kids of all ages. The Omaha riverfront's popularity for concerts and summer festivals puts the Kerrey Bridge in the spotlight as the main attraction in the area.

705 Riverfront Dr.
Omaha, NE 68102
www.visitomaha.com/bob

FUN FACT
Bob has his own Twitter account @BobTBridge

SEARCHING FOR
THE GREAT PUMPKIN

Looking for the Great Pumpkin, Charlie Brown? Well, you won't find him at Vala's Pumpkin Patch, but you will find lots of fun, gobs of food, and, yes, pumpkins. The 30-year-old pumpkin farm attracts thousands of people, who enjoy taking a hayrack ride out to the fields to pick a fresh gourd. Plenty of food options also await pumpkin hunters. Visitors can indulge in hot dogs and s'mores while huddled around a campfire on a crisp fall evening. Though most attractions, shows, and rides target families with small children, many options are available for all ages, such as a corn maze, pig races, pumpkin tosses, and miniature golf. A trip to Vala's makes for a fun date night. The Omaha area has several pumpkin patches, but Vala's does it bigger and better than anyplace else.

Vala's Pumpkin Patch
12102 S 180th St.
Gretna, NE 68028
(402) 332-4200
www.valaspumpkinpatch.com

Bellevue Berry & Pumpkin Farm
11001 South 48th St.
Papillion, NE 68133
www.bellevueberryfarm.com

Wenninghoff Farm
6707 Wenninghoff Rd.
Omaha, NE 68122
www.wenninghoff.com

WATER OFF YOUR BACK

Home to one of the country's largest water slides, Fun-Plex started with a few go-karts and grew into Nebraska's largest amusement park. Rockin' Rapids stands more than five stories high and features 1,200 feet of slides. Started as "The Kart Ranch" in the 1970s, park owners eventually added miniature golf and arcade games. Changing its name to Fun-Plex, the amusement park took off during the 1980s and continued growing. Water attractions, including Motion Ocean and giant water slides, continued to attract fans. As Fun-Plex added amusement rides, it became home to the only roller coaster in Nebraska. The "Big Ohhhhhh!!!" ended its run in 2016. Fun-Plex underwent a major expansion a few years ago to add additional water attractions, creating the largest water park in the state. Fun-Plex also opens the park for company picnics and birthday parties.

7003 Q St.
Omaha, NE 68117
(402) 331-8436
www.fun-plex.com

RECESS
TIME

Children of all ages love to bring a piece of waxed paper and to take a joy ride down the slides at Gene Leahy Pedestrian Mall. Going down the big slide, the waxed paper builds speed and sends you flying through the air for a short distance as you glide over the middle hump. The slides' popularity creates lines year-round, but they move fast. After you're done playing on the slides, grab some bread and head to the lagoon to feed the ducks and geese. While the slides may be the most popular spot at the mall, you can also enjoy a walk among the public art that hugs the path around Gene Leahy's manmade waterfalls and lagoon, which flow into the lake at the Heartland of America Park.

1302 Farnam St.
Omaha, NE 68102
(402) 444-5900
www.omaha.net/places/gene-leahy-mall

CULTURE AND HISTORY

RIDE THE RAILS
TO OMAHA'S HISTORY

The Durham Museum provides a unique perspective into local history. The Great Hall resembles the former Union Station, which hosted about ten thousand rail travelers daily from 1931 to 1971. The terminal features statues to highlight timeperiods—a soldier and sailor visiting between trains, a young woman moving to a new city, and a business executive on his way home. Union Station's architecture features an art deco design, with high ceilings, 13-foot tall chandeliers, and traditionally designed tile floors. Benches offer visitors a chance to sit and observe the beauty and history of the museum. The Durham—a museum since the mid1970s—tells Omaha's history through a series of exhibits on its lower level, including when it hosted the 1898 Trans-Mississippi Exposition (World's Fair). Visitors can also explore the area's Western heritage through Native American and pioneer displays.

801 S 10th St.
Omaha, NE 68108
(402) 444-5071
www.durhammuseum.org

HE AIN'T HEAVY,
HE'S MY BROTHER

An Academy Award statuette stands among the historical items at Boys Town's Hall of History. Donated by actor Spencer Tracy for his Oscar-winning role as Father Flanagan in the 1938 movie Boys Town, the award is one of several pieces of memorabilia highlighting the institution's national impact. The museum traces Boys Town's history from its beginning in 1917 as a group home for wayward boys to its barnstorming days, when athletic teams traveled the country to compete. Each of the four hundred students enrolled at the Boys Town school lives with an on-campus family. Boys Town celebrates Father Flanagan's influence throughout the year, including decorating his home for an old-fashioned Irish Christmas. The village has the world's largest ball of stamps, a record that has stood since 1955.

14100 Crawford St.
Boys Town, NE 68010
(402) 498-1300
www.boystown.org

FUN FACT
Father Flanagan has been considered for sainthood
with the Catholic Church.

EXPLORE DUNDEE'S
FOOD AND HISTORY

As Omaha's original suburb, Dundee's claim to fame includes an enemy attack during World War II. Japan launched firebombs targeted for the western United States. The neighborhood witnessed a firebomb explode overhead late in the war. Fortunately, the area didn't suffer any damage, and no one was hurt. As time went on and the area grew, one resident gained international fame as one of the richest men in the world. Warren Buffett calls the Happy Hollow area of Dundee home. Visitors also enjoy excellent dining options, e.g., an intimate setting with Matt's Bistro, enjoy a delicious pie at Pitch Pizza, or grab Dundee Dell's famous fish and chips. Afterward, dessert requires a stop at eCreamery, one of Omaha's best-known ice cream shops. Dundee's story includes a spot on the National Register of Historic Places.

www.dundee-memorialpark.org

HIPSTERVILLE

Benson rates as one of Omaha's most vibrant and eclectic neighborhoods, originally established as its own town in 1887 by a businessman with ties to Einstein. Nowadays, thousands of people flock to Benson on the "First Friday" of each month, as businesses stay open later and offer specials to attract people to the neighborhood. Benson offers visitors unique art galleries, restaurants, stores, and bars. You can grab a beer and find a pinball machine for a fun time at Beercade. If locally made beer lights your fire, then dinner at Benson Brewery is a must, which brews excellent beer and offers a delicious menu. If you're a street art fan, several murals cover the backs of buildings along a four-block alleyway.

www.bensonneighbors.org

OMAHA'S
MELTING POT

Call South Omaha the city's "melting pot." Enjoying the cultural influence of such nationalities as Lithuanian, Polish, Irish, German, Czech, Latino, and others, ethnic diversity highlights the area. As a result, South Omaha features some of the best ethnic celebrations in Omaha, with Cinco de Mayo topping the list. The Mexican celebration typically covers a three-day weekend, featuring a colorful parade, great food, music, and carnival rides. Another major event celebrates Santa Lucia. Omaha's Italian society celebrates its heritage with some of the best pasta and sausage and peppers around as well as a parade of a statue of Saint Lucia through the area.

www.visitomaha.com/things-to-do/entertaining-neighborhoods/south-omaha

---

TIP
For authentic Mexican food, stop by Jacobo's market.
The homemade salsa is worth the wait in line.

ALL THAT
JAZZ

Omaha's 24th and Lake Streets area has seen its share of history, but its role in Omaha's music tops the list. The epicenter for Omaha's early music scene, jazz clubs owned the "The Deuce"— as old timers know the neighborhood—during the 1920s and 1930s. Blues and jazz greats, such as Count Basie, Duke Ellington, and Nat King Cole, performed at local clubs. Omaha's dance clubs included such names as the Carnation Room, Dreamland Ballroom, and the Showcase. Listed on the National Register of Historic Places, the Dreamland Ballroom was on the second floor of the Jewell Building. The owner put up a stage and provided ample space for dancing. Local music legends Preston Love and Buddy Miles got their start here. Today, Love's Jazz and Arts Center keeps the area's love for jazz alive.

www.ljac.org

FUN FACT
Buddy Miles lent his voice as the lead singer for the "California Raisins" commercials and television specials.

THE SPIRIT OF OMAHA
LIVES ON

The Who's Who of Omaha call Prospect Hill Cemetery their final resting place. With its first burial in 1858 of a Territory senator, Prospect Hill became the cemetery for Omaha's elite. These are the people, such as Millard and Hitchcock, whose names appear on buildings, streets, and parks around Omaha. Prospect Hill's most infamous residents include a gambler and a madam. Dan Allen and Anna Wilson enjoyed a long-term relationship. Allen enjoyed life as a member of the upper class, while Wilson operated a brothel. She became wealthy based on investments from overhearing her customers talk. Allen passed in 1870 and was buried at Prospect Hill. Wilson feared her body would be dug up and moved after her burial, so she instructed that her grave be filled with concrete. Today, the couple remains at the cemetery.

3202 Parker St.
Omaha, NE 68111
(402) 556-6057
www.prospecthill-omaha.org

OMAHA'S ROYAL
FAMILY

Built in 1903, "royalty" came to Omaha with Joslyn Castle. George and Sarah Joslyn moved from Vermont to Omaha near the turn of the twentieth century. They designed their home to resemble a Scottish castle, with the Scottish thistle image worked into walls and light fixtures. The Joslyns named the 35-room Baronial mansion "Lyndhurst," but locals preferred to call it Joslyn Castle, as if Omaha's "royal" family lived there. The mansion survived a major tornado that hit Omaha in 1913, which killed about 150 people citywide. While the castle sustained little damage, the landscaped grounds didn't fare as well. The Joslyn family lived in the mansion until 1940, when the estate donated it to the city of Omaha following Sarah's death. George had passed in 1916. Omaha Public Schools used the castle as offices for several years. Today, the castle operates as part of a trust and offers monthly tours of the facility.

3902 Davenport St.
Omaha, NE 68131
(402) 595-2199
www.joslyncastle.com

MODERN ART
WITH A FLAIR

Imagine hundreds of Hawaiian shirts hanging from wires in a large exhibit hall. Or maybe tapestries depicting life under Nazi rule for Jewish people. Creativity and imagination drive exhibits at the Kaneko Art Gallery. Opened in 1998, the gallery presents exhibits with themes, such as fabric, water, and motion, and does not charge admission. The gallery focuses on contemporary art while challenging people to think about what they're seeing or feeling. Located in former warehouses near the Old Market, the Kaneko attracts diverse groups of visitors. Cofounder and artist Jun Kaneko was born in Japan and studied at the California Institute of Art and the University of California. He later moved to Omaha in 1986, where his work includes pieces known as Dangos (abstract sculptures), which are displayed nationally.

1111 Jones St.
Omaha, NE 68102
(402)341-3800
www.thekaneko.org

WINTER
IN OMAHA

During the westward expansion in the 1800s, Omaha served as the winter home for Mormons trekking to Salt Lake City, Utah. As the pioneers traveled, the Mormon Trail cut through most of Nebraska. Forced from their homes in Nauvoo, Illinois, Mormons sought refuge in Salt Lake. Due to the treacherous traveling conditions, however, Omaha became the winter headquarters for the pioneers, who would spend up to two years in the area while they earned money to replenish their supplies. Visit the Mormon Trail Center at Historic Winter Quarters to learn their stories and reflect on the history of the pioneers' struggles and the development of Omaha, including creating the town of Florence. Mormon influence continues with a temple and pioneer cemetery near the museum.

3215 State St.
Omaha, NE 68112
(402) 453-9372
www.lds.org/locations/mormon-trail-center-at-historic-winter-quarters

FUN FACT
The area's largest gingerbread house exhibit is held every December at the visitors center.

GO WITH
THE FLO

Taking advantage of the abandoned buildings of the Mormon winter quarters, investors founded the town of Florence in 1854. The Florence Bank opened two years later—this oldest building in Omaha now serves as a museum. The town enjoyed its heyday during its early years, even serving as the illegal site of the Territorial legislature for a day as arguments ensued on where the permanent capitol should be located. Unable to grow larger than a small town, Omaha annexed the area in 1917. While the Mormons abandoned their winter site, the church's influence remains in the area. The Mormon Trail Center at Historic Winter Quarters tells the story of the move westward to Utah, including the years in Omaha. During their time here, Brigham Young supervised construction of many buildings, including the Florence Mill, which now serves as a museum.

CRUISE AMERICA'S
MAIN STREET

U.S. Highway 30—aka the Lincoln Highway—runs across the northern half of the United States. Built in 1913, US 30 served as America's first transcontinental highway. Communities competed to be included as part of the initial highway. US 30 ran through Omaha along Dodge Street, near downtown. A section of highway included a brick road between Omaha and nearby Elkhorn. Eventually, officials rerouted Highway 30 around Omaha, but the city sought to keep a mile-long section of the Elkhorn brick road open. Named to the National Register of Historic Places in 1984, people still drive on this road except for winter months, when Omaha strives to protect it from potential damage caused by snow blades used by trucks clearing the road.

Old Lincoln Highway
Elkhorn, NE 68022
lincolnhighwaynebraskabyway.com

BE A
CURATOR

Open for more than eighty years, the Joslyn Museum's collections range from ancient Egypt to contemporary art, with most artwork hailing from the eighteenth and nineteenth centuries. A Rembrandt painting from 1658 is one of the oldest works in the European collection. Since Omaha is considered the gateway to the West, it seems appropriate that Joslyn's collection includes Western art and Native American exhibits. Western art features works by Karl Bodmer and Frederic Remington, while Oscar Howe represents the Native American artists. Outside the museum, about twenty pieces await you during a stroll through the sculpture garden. While the museum offers free admission to its permanent collections, it charges a small fee for special exhibitions, such as traveling displays.

2200 Dodge St.
Omaha, NE 68102
(402) 342-3300
www.joslyn.org

HONOR
TRIBAL CULTURE

The grounds of Metropolitan Community College once held Ponca Chief Standing Bear and his followers prisoner. Today, the college hosts the annual Fort Omaha Intertribal Powwow every September. Dancers gather to honor the history, tradition, customs, and art of the state's tribes—Ponca, Winnebago, Omaha, and Santee Sioux. Dancers compete in a variety of dances, such as traditional grass, shawl, fancy, and jingle. The powwow dancers' regalia feature vibrant colors. Each song performed by tribal drum groups tells a story, ranging from military service to traditional buffalo hunts. While the music is at the forefront of the powwow, food is abundant. Indian tacos—taco ingredients atop a plate-sized frybread—rank high on the list of favorite powwow foods. Handmade jewelry and accessories are available from Native vendors. The Fort Omaha powwow closes the dance season in Nebraska.

5300 N 30th St.
Omaha, NE 68111
(531) 622-2400
www.mccneb.edu

BE THE
ART

The Old Market includes buildings that are more than a century old, so it seems oddly fitting that an aged building would showcase contemporary art. Opened in the early 1980s, the Bemis Center for Contemporary Arts highlights the work of young contemporary artists. Visitors stroll through makeshift galleries inside the brick façade, viewing exhibits that range from paintings to interactive video or music pieces. It's rare to see the same artist's work more than once, as the pieces rotate through an artist-in-residence program. The Bemis supports art by offering programs encouraging public participation. The 1887 building was named to the National Register of Historic Places in 1985, and once housed the Bemis Bag Company.

724 S 12th St.
Omaha, NE 68102
(402) 341-7130
www.bemiscenter.org

BUILD A
FORT

Looking out from the guardhouse, prairie grass taller than a human stretches for miles, like an ocean. This view likely greeted soldiers first stationed at Fort Atkinson, the first fort built west of the Missouri River, where more than a thousand soldiers maintained peace between fur traders and local Native American tribes between 1820 and 1827. Explorer William Clark recommended its location following meetings between the Lewis and Clark Expedition and tribal leaders in 1804 at a spot near the current fort. The army abandoned Fort Atkinson in the late 1820s following new assignments. After falling into disrepair and eventually becoming farmland, the Nebraska state park system purchased the land and started rebuilding the fort beginning in the 1960s. Today, reenactors gather during summer months to relive 1800s life at the fort.

201 S 7th St.
Fort Calhoun, NE 68023
(402) 468-5895
www.fortatkinsononline.org

LEARN ABOUT
MALCOLM X

Born Malcolm Little, the son of a Christian minister would grow up to become Malcolm X, one of the most profound and eloquent speakers of the Civil Rights era. The Littles left Omaha shortly before Malcolm's first birthday in 1926 to avoid attacks by the Ku Klux Klan. The house where Malcolm lived as a baby is gone, but the location has been honored by the state with a historical marker, surrounded by a small plaza. The Malcolm X Foundation owns the property. As a young man, Malcolm found his following with the Nation of Islam, later becoming Sunni Muslim. He adopted the name el-Hajj Malik el-Shabazz. Known simply as Malcolm X, he led a movement during the early 1960s for social justice for African Americans. Members of the Nation of Islam assassinated Malcolm X in 1965 at the age of 39.

3448 Evans St.
Omaha, NE 68111
(402) 881-8118
www.malcolmfoundation.org

HEAR THE
BELLS

Bells ring out, signaling that mass has started at Omaha's Roman Catholic cathedral. Standing more than 200' tall, people easily recognize the twin bell towers at St. Cecilia Cathedral, which is perched atop a hill in central Omaha. The home of the Roman Catholic Archdiocese of Omaha, the cathedral's bell towers have only been part of the church since 1958. St. Cecilia held its first mass in 1916. The cathedral presents a unique appearance, with a mix of Spanish and Italian Renaissance styles. The main exterior uses the Spanish style, while the bell towers and interior feature the Italian Renaissance, including window columns and frames. For more than three decades, St. Cecilia has hosted a flower festival every January, which unites artists and florists to create displays based on the festival's theme, such as Nebraska's 150th birthday or films.

701 N 40th St.
Omaha, NE 68131
(402) 551-2313
www.stceciliacathedral.org

CHECK OUT THE LIBRARY
OF THE FUTURE

You don't need to know the Dewey Decimal System to enjoy this library. It seems fitting that Omaha's digital library sits in a former bookstore. Instead of checking out a book, visitors can check out a seat and plug in their laptop or tablet to work or surf the Internet. Visitors conducting research can access digital archives through Do Space's partnership with the Omaha Public Library system. As technology improves, Do Space offers an opportunity for product development using its 3D lab. Visitors can also learn a variety of coding and develop relationships with mentors. Do Space encourages tech education with children, featuring a play area with interactive exhibits. In the tradition of the old bookstore, if you just want to read a book, the tech center offers a collection of e-books.

7205 Dodge St.
Omaha, NE 68114
(402) 819-4022
www.dospace.org

CELEBRATE THE FOURTH
WITH A CONCERT

Thousands fill the park's massive green space, creating an eclectic checkerboard of blankets and lawn chairs. As soon as the band hits its first note, fans rise and sing along to almost every hit song performed by some of the best classic pop music artists. Omaha kicks off the Independence Day celebration with its annual "Celebrate America" festival at Memorial Park. The event includes food and drink, as concert-goers celebrate the nation's birthday listening to performances by such artists as Huey Lewis, Kenny Loggins, and Kool and the Gang. A fireworks show caps the celebration. Memorial Park serves as the perfect backdrop for the event, as it honors the men and women who served in America's wars.

6005 Underwood Ave.
Omaha, NE 68132
(402) 444-5955
www.parks.cityofomaha.org

LEARN ABOUT AMERICA'S
COLD WAR

America's strategic defense ran through Omaha at one time. Offutt Air Force Base hosted the Strategic Air Command headquarters for forty-five years. The end of the Cold War shifted national concerns, eliminating SAC's role in 1992 and replacing it with the Strategic Command, also located at Offutt. SAC lives on, however, with a museum dedicated to its memory. The SAC and Aerospace Museum, about a 20-minute drive from the city, recognizes the role the Air Force had in protecting the United States during a critical period. The museum uses aircraft, such as a B-52 bomber and F-4 Phantom fighter, as well as missiles and other memorabilia to tell the Cold War story. The museum also includes exhibits on space exploration, featuring an Apollo command module. Additionally, the museum highlights the story of Clayton Anderson, Nebraska's lone astronaut.

28210 W Park Hwy.
Ashland, NE 68003
(402) 944-3100
www.sacmuseum.org

FUN FACT
The SAC Museum was originally an outdoor exhibit at Offutt, but community leaders wanted a new facility to keep aircraft from rusting.

LITTLE CHAPEL
ON THE PRAIRIE

Call it the little chapel on the prairie. Most people driving along Interstate 80 west of Omaha likely wonder why a church sits atop a hill surrounded by cornfields. Open since 2002, the Holy Family Shrine attracts about twenty thousand people annually, some wanting a spiritual connection, while others just want to visit. The shrine offers a breathtaking architectural design, with wood arches resembling waves of grain. The glass walls stretch 49', with a portrait of the holy family etched in the northern wall. The interior also radiates beauty, highlighted with natural lighting. A 40' stainless steel cross identifies the shrine as Catholic. A visitors center traces its origins, as it recognizes the Catholic faith.

23132 Pflug Rd.
Gretna, NE 68028
(402) 332-4565
www.holyfamilyshrineproject.com

ART
BECKONS

Omaha has embraced public art, with sculptures and murals sprouting up around the city. Murals especially tell an area's story, and buildings offer a natural canvas. Fertile Ground, Omaha's best-known mural, traces the city's history from its early days to the present. Completed in 2008, the artist, muralist Meg Saligman, photographed fifty people to include in the 32,500-square-foot mural on the Energy Systems building across from TD Ameritrade Park. South Omaha features a half block of murals, with each telling the story of Hispanic culture and history, including Pancho Villa. A few blocks west, the Lithuanian Bakery is home to a mural highlighting the Eastern European country's influence. In north Omaha, murals also share the history of African American influence in the area, including Omaha native Malcolm X.

www.publicartomaha.org

TIP
Check out the Benson neighborhood for some unique street art in the alleys, including a take on Donkey Kong.

AN IMMIGRANT
STORY

Polka, kolaches, and marionettes help tell the story of Omaha's Czech-Slovak community. Opened in 2014 inside a former restaurant at the Crossroads Mall, the Czech-Slovak Museum offers a look at the group's immigration to the Midwest. Czechs and Slovaks started settling in the Omaha area during the 1860s. Polka music remains a stronghold of the Czech culture, and no one defined Midwestern polka better than Moostash Joe. The bandleader hosted a Sunday afternoon polka show on a local radio station for almost 60 years. As you tour the museum, grab a tasty kolache, which features a dollop of fruit inside a pastry. The museum features a display with marionettes and puppets because they have been historically important in highlighting Czech-Slovak culture through performances.

7400 Dodge St., Ste. D11A
Omaha, NE 68114
(402) 686-9837
www.czechandslovakmuseum.org

Other local history museums:

Great Plains Black History Museum
2221 N 24th St.
Omaha, NE 68110
(402) 401-9893

Sarpy County Musuem
2402 Clay St.
Bellevue, NE 68005
(402) 292-1880
sarpycountymuseum.org

Washington County Museum
102 N 14th St.
Fort Calhoun, NE 68023
(402) 468-5740
www.wchamuseum.com

HONEST ABE'S
RAILROAD

Omaha can thank President Abraham Lincoln for helping it to become the home of Union Pacific, the nation's largest railroad company. With the president's backing, Omaha beat out neighbor Council Bluffs to serve as the eastern terminus of the new railroad built during the 1860s. Today, Union Pacific's headquarters calls downtown Omaha home, but the railroad's story is told at the Union Pacific Railroad Museum in Council Bluffs. The three-story museum traces the railroad's story, from Lincoln's support to present-day operations, including an engine simulator where people can drive a train around a mountain. The two cities unite each summer for Railroad Days, a two-day festival that offers free admission to five locations related to rail history, including the General Dodge house, home to the soldier assigned to oversee the railroad's construction.

200 Pearl St.
Council Bluffs, IA
(712) 329-8307
www.upmuseum.org

BIRTHPLACE OF A
PRESIDENT

Born Leslie King Jr., the young man grew up to make American history. Less than a month after his birth, Gerald Ford's mother moved the family to Michigan and later divorced his father. His mother remarried, and the new father adopted the young boy, changing his name to Gerald R. Ford. As a Congressional representative from Michigan, Ford made history when he served as the nation's first nonelected vice president and president following the Watergate scandal in the early 1970s. He eventually lost the 1976 presidential election to Jimmy Carter. Omaha sought to honor the 38th president by recognizing his birthplace, but a fire destroyed the house. In its place rose the Gerald R. Ford Birthsite and Gardens. The memorial includes monuments and statues honoring President Ford as well as other presidents and former Nebraska governors.

3202 Woolworth Ave.
Omaha, NE 68105
(402) 444-5955
www.nebraskahistory.org/conserve/birthsite.htm

BECOME A
PIONEER

Nebraskans' "pioneer spirit" recognizes the determination and strong work ethic locals take pride in. First National's Spirit of Nebraska's Wilderness and Pioneer Courage Park honors the pioneers' westward move in the 1800s with life-sized statues, including a trail boss atop his steed overlooking the wagon trail. The exhibit then encourages visitors to walk the five-block route and imagine life on the Oregon and Mormon Trails. The art project also provides interesting pieces, including bison sculptures placed on the sides of buildings, giving the illusion they're moving in and out of the structures. The sculpture walk then concludes with bison appearing to run onto a field near a fountain featuring spooked Canadian geese statues taking flight.

www.firstnational.com/site/about-us/in-the-community/sculpture-parks.fhtml

STOP
THE PRESSES

Mildred Brown used her role as the owner and publisher of the Omaha Star to promote and lead her community. Brown started the African American weekly newspaper in 1938 with her husband. They divorced a few years later. She kept the newspaper, which is believed to have been the longest-running weekly newspaper in the United States owned by an African American woman. Brown passed away in 1989, but the paper lives on, currently in the hands of a niece. Brown lived in an apartment above the office while running the newspaper. Brown used the paper to support the Civil Rights movement in Omaha, giving a voice to the oppressed. In appreciation for her accomplishments, the Omaha Business Hall of Fame honored Brown with a posthumous induction. The Omaha Star's building is also listed on the National Register of Historic Places.

2216 N 24th St.
Omaha, NE 68110
(402) 346-4041
www.theomahastar.com

THE GENERAL'S
QUARTERS

A Civil War veteran, General George Crook earned a reputation as a respected and feared soldier during the Indian Wars of the late 1800s. Fort Omaha opened in 1868 as Sherman Barracks, a supply stop for the military. Assigned as the fort's commander in the mid-1870s, the Army built a new house for General Crook's use. He opposed anything elaborate, so the brick house featured moderate amenities. The general worked out of the home, so his office was spacious enough for staff meetings. He and Mrs. Crook also slept in separate bedrooms so that the general could be accessible to his team. Today, visitors can stroll through the house atop a hill overlooking the parade grounds on the campus of a local community college. The college maintains the fort's original buildings.

5730 N 30th St.
Omaha, NE 68111
(402) 455-9990
www.douglascohistory.org

EXPLORE
YOUR ARTSY SIDE

Take an old mattress factory, mix in about eighty artists, and shake well. Voilà! You have Omaha's Hot Shops Art Center. The North Downtown (NoDo) collective features artists dabbling in anything from photography and oil painting to pottery and glass blowing. Four studios focusing on heat-related art—Bruning Sculpture, CK Fabrication, Crystal Forge, and Hot Shops Pottery—anchor Hot Shops. Artists have also created some of Omaha's best-known statues and art exhibits, such as the giant O! Man near the Old Market. Opened in 1999, its location and eclectic artists make Hot Shops a unique experience. Strolling through the three-story building allows visitors an opportunity to witness the range of art that exists in Omaha. Artists interact with visitors, sharing their experiences and hosting classes.

1301 Nicholas St.
Omaha, NE 68102
(402) 342-6452
www.hotshopsartcenter.com

BE A BILLIONAIRE
FOR A DAY

Berkshire Hathaway hosts its annual stockholders meeting in downtown Omaha, attracting thousands of visitors every spring. You can follow the footsteps of Warren Buffett, one of the richest men in the world, who calls Omaha home. Buffett's holding company—Berkshire Hathaway—is headquartered in Omaha. He conducts meetings near his corner office at the Kiewit Building in the Midtown Crossing district. Or you can check out some spots where you might see the "Oracle of Omaha," as Buffett is known, such as Nebraska Furniture Mart, the world's largest furniture store. Buffett's company bought the franchise in 1983. You can also grab dinner at Gorat's steakhouse, which is a favorite dining spot for Buffett, who's known for bringing celebrity guests with him. Take a drive through the Happy Hollow neighborhood, where Buffett has lived since buying his home there in the 1950s.

ENJOY
YOUR STAY

Omaha's Magnolia Hotel offers guests upscale service while providing a boutique-hotel experience. The hotel targets business travel during the week and couples on the weekend. The hotel's 145 guest rooms and 12 two-level suites provide visitors a great experience, with comfortable beds and interesting décor, featuring Tennessee marble flooring in the lobby area and Brazilian cherry wood. The 4-floor hotel sits in the old Aquila Court building. Named in honor of his grandmother, the Aquila was built in 1923 by Chicago financier Chester Cook. The building joined the National Register of Historic Places in 1974. Because of its downtown location, the Magnolia offers proximity to attractions, including the Orpheum Theater. Cast members from shows at the Orpheum often stay at the Magnolia. Most attractions, such as the popular Old Market, are within walking distance of the hotel, but shuttle service is available. What's the best part of staying at the Magnolia? It may be the nightly cookies and milk.

1615 Howard St.
Omaha, NE 68102
(402) 341-2500
www.magnoliahotelomaha.com

LEARN
WHILE YOU PLAY

At the Omaha Children's Museum, children mix learning with play, such as learning about cars at the Walker Tire garage, banking at the Imagination Lab, or science at the technology center. Youngsters' imaginations come to life as they work on new creations in the Tinker Lab. The Omaha Children's Museum is home to the old Richman Gordman department store's Zooland play area, a childhood memory for many parents and grandparents, dating to the 1960s. Children can climb and play on a set of four large animal-designed figures as their parents once did at the old department stores.

500 S 20th St.
Omaha, NE 68102
(402) 342-6164
www.ocm.org

IN THE
NAVY

Known as the headquarters of the old Strategic Air Command, Omaha also features a naval arsenal attraction. Vessels that once sailed the high seas call Freedom Park home. The naval influence started with the *USS Hazard,* which operated as a minesweeper in the Pacific Ocean during World War II. The ship was taken out of mothballs and donated to the city of Omaha about forty years ago. Nearby, the *USS Marlin,* one of the smallest submarines built for the Navy, stands guard following her days as a Cold War training vessel. Freedom Park nearly met its demise in 2011 when a major flood damaged several of the exhibits, including aircraft and anti-aircraft guns, but volunteers worked with the city to refurbish the park and its displays.

2497 Freedom Park Rd.
Omaha, NE 68110
(402) 444-5955
www.cityofomaha.org

INTO THE
WILD BLUE YONDER

At an airshow at Offutt Air Force Base, more than a hundred thousand people stand in unison, eyes pointed skyward, watching for that first glimpse. Then, seemingly out of nowhere, they appear, flying at speeds beyond belief, inches apart. Patriotic colors of red, white, and blue spew from behind them, and the jets make an acrobatic move that leaves the crowd cheering in amazement. The air show hosts elite aerobatic flying teams, such as the Air Force's Thunderbirds and the Navy's Blue Angels. The two-day event also offers visitors aerial displays and skydivers, among air battle reenactments. On the ground, people scour the stationary displays getting as close as possible to some of the aircraft they usually see only on television or movies—bombers, fighters, cargo planes, and helicopters.

109 Washington Square
Offutt Air Force Base, NE 68113
(402) 294-1110
www.offutt.af.mil

NATIVE
AMERICAN VICTORY

When it opened in the late 1860s, no one could foresee that Fort Omaha would become the site of a landmark legal decision. A few years later, Ponca Chief Standing Bear wanted to bury his son on their tribal homeland in northeastern Nebraska after the tribe had been relocated to an Oklahoma reservation. During their travels north, the Army arrested the Poncas for leaving without permission. Awaiting trial, Standing Bear was held by the Army at Fort Omaha. Believing the chief had the right to bury his son in Nebraska, an Omaha attorney sued the federal government. Having befriended Standing Bear, General George Crook— the fort's commander—testified on his behalf, which helped persuade the judge. In the end, the 1879 trial declared Native Americans human beings under the law. Today, a historical marker recognizes the event near the fort's parade grounds.

5300 N 30th St.
Omaha, NE 68111
(531) 622-2400
www.mccneb.edu

SHOPPING AND FASHION

WELCOME TO OMAHA'S
ORIGINAL DOWNTOWN

Once the hub for wholesale and retail shopping for early-day Omaha, today's Old Market mixes the flavor of the past with contemporary lifestyles. Omaha's original downtown serves as a retail and entertainment district where visitors can find all sorts of things to satisfy their interests. Brick-laid streets spark memories of earlier times, while century-old buildings are homes to businesses and condominiums. Several buildings maintain their late 1800s designs with cast-iron windowsills and sloped entryways, which helped the district to be named to the National Register of Historic Places. During the day, the Old Market welcomes families and couples seeking a good meal, shopping, and enjoying museums and art galleries. At night, the nine-square block district takes on a new vibe, entertaining a younger crowd in the bars and clubs.

www.oldmarket.com

SHOP
TIL YOU DROP

Omahans used to drive to Kansas City to shop at such stores as Michael Kors, Coach, Brooks Brothers, and Ralph Lauren. That's history, though, as these stores are among seventy-two calling the Nebraska Crossing Outlets home, about a 20-minute drive outside Omaha near Gretna. Opened in 2013, the outdoor shopping center immediately caught on with shoppers looking for bargains, with the parking lots routinely packed. Affordable options, including Chico's, American Eagle, and Columbia, join the upscale businesses to attract a diverse clientele. Besides clothing stores, shoppers can find deals at specialty stores Bose, Claire's, GNC, and Fossil, among others. If you work up an appetite while shopping, check out one of the eight eateries, including local favorites Voodoo Taco and Local Beer, Patio and Kitchen.

21209 Nebraska Crossing Dr.
Gretna, NE 68028
(402) 332-5650
www.nexoutlets.com

ANTIQUE,
OMAHA STYLE

One person's junk is another person's gold. Or so it would appear for antique shopping. A popular "sport" in Omaha, about two dozen stores seek to help make people's dreams come true. Six of these stores call the popular Old Market area home. The Antique Annex encourages visitors to check out its stores with a series of old record albums nailed on a short boardwalk near the entrance. Inside, visitors find almost anything they can imagine, from an old typewriter with a ribbon still in it to 1950s poodle skirts. The Imaginarium holds so many antiques that it needs two stores to sell its wares, including the Imaginarium Super Store. Antique stores attract visitors all over Omaha, including MishMash in the Benson neighborhood. Describing itself as a "thriftique," the store sells both antiques and collectibles.

FRESH FOOD
IN THE CITY

While Omaha hosts several seasonal markets, the Farmers Market has called the Old Market home since 1994, following a 30-year absence. Nowadays, you can find delicious fruits and vegetables at the Farmers Market, even organic ones. Also on the menu is people-watching. Couples of all ages, some with cute dogs on stylish leashes, and families of all backgrounds snugly gather in a one-block area, just feet away from where early Omahans bought their supplies in the Old Market, which was then the city's main shopping district. Today's shoppers sample locally produced wine and beer or homemade bread and meats. Market-goers browse while entertained by street musicians and balloon artists. The market, featuring about one hundred vendors, offers a variety of local products. Shoppers can come for tomatoes and go home with amazing enchiladas or stone-fired pizza.

519 S 11th St.
Omaha, NE 68102
(402) 345-5401
www.omahafarmersmarket.com

TAKE A TRIP
DOWN NOSTALGIA LANE

If you're a fan of nostalgia, then Hollywood Candy needs to be on your Omaha bucket list. It's home to an eclectic collection of nostalgic candy, soda, and movie-themed memorabilia. The store has a large collection of sweets, including taffy, jellies, and lollipops—even Willy Wonka candy—and whether you call it pop, soda, or something else, there's lots of it, from Dad's Root Beer to odd ones, such as bacon-flavored soda. Walk past the candy and you'll spy Pez dispensers. Hollywood Candy's Pez collection rivals anyone's. If you like nostalgic metal lunch boxes, you also have a wide selection from which to choose. Want to invite friends over for your own movie screening? You can rent the store's theater for a couple of hours to watch your own DVD. Afterward, you can take a break and grab a treat at the on-site soda fountain.

1209 Jackson St.
Omaha, NE 68102
(402) 346-9746
www.hollywoodcandy.com

EXPLORE
AN OLD ALLEY

Omaha's Old Market offers a diverse area of shopping, dining, and entertainment. The area attracts all demographics a business could want. During the day and evening, families and couples mill about the shops and restaurants. With the young bar crowd in the late night, the Old Market becomes a people-watching extravaganza. The Old Market also has smaller enclaves, each offering its own unique appeal. The Old Market Passageway features a variety of interests, including Mexican food and steak dinners, international clothing, and curiosity items at stores. You can browse a litany of books and check out an array of artwork. Astrology followers enjoy the Garden of the Zodiac and the busts recognizing each of the astrological signs. The one-time alley developed into The Passageway about three decades ago.

417 S 11th St.
Omaha, NE 68102
(402) 341-1910
www.passagewaygallery.com

NATURAL BEAUTY

SMELL
THE FLOWERS

Stop and smell the flowers at Lauritzen Gardens. Opened in 1982, Lauritzen features almost twenty gardens spread out over a hundred acres. As you stroll through the grounds, make sure you visit the Rose Garden, which features dozens of types of roses and about two thousand plants. Lauritzen features additional gardens, such as the English perennial, children's, herb, and Japanese. The garden even has the world's largest outdoor train set. Added in 2015, the conservatory offers visitors a chance to view tropical and temperate plants and flowers in an enclosed environment. Resembling a large greenhouse, the conservatory also hosts seasonal exhibits, such as glass art and Lego animals. While the gardens are popular year-round, people love Lauritzen's special events, including the holiday poinsettia show featuring more than five thousand poinsettias and a 25-foot tall tree made of poinsettias.

100 Bancroft St.
Omaha, NE 68108
(402) 346-4002
www.lauritzengardens.org

TAKE A
WALK

Walking along Zorinsky Lake at sunset rates as a memorable experience in Omaha. The view of the sun setting behind the trees and the reflection in the water creates a beautiful scene. This area in west Omaha includes two trails, a 4-mile route, and a 7.5-mile path. On the lake, you'll see kayakers, stand-up paddle boaters, and fishermen. Onshore, families picnic, and children play at the playgrounds. Bicyclists and runners join the walkers along the trails. The park includes a garden, featuring native prairie grass. The nearly 1,000-acre Zorinsky Lake Park which opened in 1993, was created as part of a dam project to prevent flooding along Papio Creek. The lake's name honors former Mayor and Senator Ed Zorinsky.

Zorinsky Lake Park
3808 S 154th St.
Omaha, NE 68144
(402) 444-5900
www.parks.cityofomaha.org

Glenn Cunningham Lake
8305 Rainwood Rd., Omaha, NE 68122
(402) 444-4628
www.parks.cityofomaha.org

Standing Bear Lake
6404 N 132nd St., Omaha, NE 68164
(402) 444-4676
www.parks.cityofomaha.org

Lake Manawa
1100 S Shore Dr., Council Bluffs, IA 51501-7354
(712) 366-4802
www.iowadnr.gov

Carter Lake
Abbott Drive and Carter Lake Blvd.,
Carter Lake, IA 51510

ENJOY A DAY
IN THE PARK

Every day can feel like a Saturday in the park when you visit Heartland of America Park. Opened in 1990, the park offers visitors an opportunity to relax and enjoy the view. Gondolas glide over a small lake, while a nearby color-changing fountain shoots water more than three hundred feet into the air. Meanwhile, people lounge, some lying on the manicured green grass, reading a book or just enjoying a sunny day. Families can be seen feeding bits of bread to ducks and geese. Heartland of America Park recognizes Omaha's history, with exhibits highlighting industry and movie stars from the area, including Marlon Brando, Henry Fonda, and Nick Nolte. A beautiful statue tells the story of World War II and its impact on the battlefield and the home front. The park also anchors the annual Taste of Omaha food festival.

www.visitomaha.com/listings/heartland-of-america-park-and-fountain/56947

TAKE
A HIKE

With seventeen miles of trails, Fontenelle Forest offers a little bit of wilderness in the city. Located along the Missouri River, hikers take in the river's view while trekking over natural paths or along the 1.5-mile long boardwalk. Hiking the trails provides an impressive day out, as you can move from the boardwalk to hilly paths, eventually traveling along the wetlands trail in the lowlands. Trails offer opportunities to view wildlife, including deer, squirrels, and great numbers of birds, such as eagles and hawks. Fontenelle Forest offers several family activities, including the Acorn Acres play area and educational programs. Besides offering nature opportunities, Fontenelle Forest rescues hundreds of birds of prey. Unable to survive in the wild, some hawks, falcons, and owls call the Raptor Wildlife Refuge home.

1111 Bellevue Blvd. N
Bellevue, NE 68005
(402) 731-3140
www.fontenelleforest.org

TIP
Bring your binoculars.
Fontenelle Forest is a great spot for bird-watching year-round.

HUG
AN ALPACA

Ever hug an alpaca? Alpacas of the Heartland is a working farm located a few miles north of Omaha. The farm's owners share their love of alpacas annually with a free open house, allowing visitors to get up close while learning about the South American animals. Or you can enjoy a glass of your favorite wine while alpacas graze nearby, as the farmers host special events, including wine tastings or yoga lessons. Bred for their fleece, these alpacas found their way to Omaha after the owners saw their first one about ten years ago. Today, about thirty-five alpacas roam the hillside farm in large pastures, with some alpacas available for sale. The farm also operates a small boutique, which features alpaca products.

7016 County Rd. 39
Fort Calhoun, NE 68023
(402) 669-6979
www.alpacasoftheheartland.com

VISIT A
GEM

Hiking, horseback riding, and camping highlight a visit to the
Eugene T. Mahoney State Park. Many activities make this "jewel"
of the state park system a year-round attraction. Besides camping
spots for RVs and tents, the park offers cabins and a lodge in which
to stay. Outdoor activities draw about a million visitors annually.
Fishing and paddle boating are available at a marina, while
children can swim at the aquatic center, featuring a waterslide.
Visitors take in the sights of the Platte River valley from a 70-foot
high observation tower. Or you can even check out a melodrama
at the park's amphitheater. The state park also offers fun winter
activities, including open areas for sledding and cross-country
skiing. Mahoney State Park access requires a paid park permit.

Eugene T. Mahoney State Park
28500 W Park Hwy.
Ashland, NE 68003
(402) 944-2523
www.nebraskastateparks.com

Platte River State Park
14421 346th St., Louisville NE 68037
(402) 234-2217
www.nebraskastateparks.com

SUGGESTED
ITINERARIES

DATE NIGHT

Dundee Theater, 36

Concert at a small venue, 45

Orpheum Theater, 40

Old Market, 114

Flatiron Cafe, 29

Hollywood Candy, 118

Soaring Wings Vineyard, 24

Bob Kerrey Pedestrian Bridge, 42

Alpine Inn, 12

Sip champagne from a tap at Homy Inn, 31

FAMILY DAY WITH THE KIDS

Henry Doorly Zoo and Aquarium, 64

Durham Museum, 74

Lee Simmons Wildlife Park, 65

Fun-Plex, 70

Slides at Gene Leahy Pedestrian Mall, 71

Orsi's Italian Bakery and Pizzeria, 19

Fontenelle Forest, 128

Children's Museum, 108

SAC Museum, 94

The Rose Theater, 47

• •

DAY AT THE PARK

SPORTS OUTING

ACTIVITIES
BY SEASON

SPRING

Walk along the Riverfront, 66

Henry Doorly Zoo and Aquarium, 64

Lee Simmons Wildlife Park, 65

Werner Park, 57

Fontenelle Forest, 128

Catch an indoor football game, 63

SUMMER

Check out a festival, 42

College World Series, 59

Soaring Wings Vineyard, 24

Fun-Plex, 70

Horsemen's Park, 62

Independence Day celebration concert at Memorial Park, 93

Get your Geek on, 41

Werner Park, 57

Ted and Wally's, 18

Lauritzen Gardens, 123

FALL

WINTER

INDEX